EARLY MUSIC

First published in 2020
by Many Rivers Press
PO Box 868
Langley, WA 98260
USA

A catalog record for this book
is available from
the Library of Congress

ISBN 978-1-932887-53-2

Printed in
the United States of America

Cover artwork *Namrata Desai*
Cover design *Julie Quiring*

EARLY MUSIC

Poems by
MÍCHEÁL Ó SÚILLEABHÁIN

MANY RIVERS PRESS
LANGLEY WASHINGTON
www.davidwhyte.com

Dedicated to my mother and father, who pursued a life illuminated.

Contents

ADMONITION

Burren Unbroken

I sit and watch the mountain
engulfed in light loneliness.
Primitive trepidation
all clarity and wonder,
shuffling my cold feet
feeling out the morning,
wondering, who would hear this
barefoot verse and find solace?
This magnum song from the rocks.

The mountain horizon
like a voice, singing
unbroken, down
to the water.

Turas d' Anam

Often times
the step backward
lets the soul catch up.
So that all our happy
hindsights harmonise
and wisdom builds.

Share your luck.
Be miserly only
with misfortune.
In each seismic
shudder we learn
to trust the ground
again, humble again,
knowingly broken,
unrepentently wounded,
proud to bare pain.

Laying claim to
the joy factory
of your body.

No more tariffs, or sanctions.
Wage cuts and glass ceilings.
Conventions, expenses paid, nor
lanyards or company position.

Often times,
this way you can live
in ways others simply
will not, develop sides
of you others simply
would not.

So feel the rhythm
beyond the beat.
Begin with a break,
and let your soul
catch up.

Let Sit

No craving strong enough
nor will of the mind more fervent.
Grateful to carry a soldered wound
burned shut mercifully,
my anvil still ringing.

Still as a thatched cottage
after heavy rain, sodden.
Yet still my hearth glows,
still remembers, buried beneath
the lightest layer of bog's ash,
half smothered, half protected,
ready to be blown back.

Taste it on your tongue,
the fine dust in the air now
embers reveal their design.
Place turf upon yesterday's
remnants, the wet bog
smokes for what seems
an unlikely lifetime.

Let sit, the fuel will spark.
So sit, and wait, and watch
bog turn to fire.

What To Hand On

I'd wish to grow wise,
through gears of existence.
To read the gradient
in each phase of life
just to coast down the slopes
beyond travailing times.

To know the right hat
for the right company, and
rhythm of each interaction,
chiming in from the periphery
to read the grain
of every conversation.

To fall in love
in the prime of life, seeds
sewn of deathbed smiles.

Waves of wellbeing
lap at lowtide, imploring
your reluctant side to break,
even one cycle learned
as a child.

For wisdom knows
what to hold, and
what to hand on.
Which to give and
what to keep.

Where to dig and
what to bury.
When to wake, and
how to sleep.
Our wish for wisdom
still a whisper,
the source of which
still buried deep.

So, soul brother, and
soul sister, are we changed
by what we meet.

A Scribbling in the Dark

As if by séance,
you have called
your life back.
It is like handwriting
in the dark, a trusting
muscle memory, an
innocent intimacy
far from the slave
driver's lash upon
the chain gang
of your soul.

Again your body
seems a medium,
a singing bowl
about to be tipped.

You first flirted, then
lay with the abyss,
staying long enough
for fear to leave you
and the choice be
fully yours.

Hate gave way to
hesitant forgiveness.
A healing forgetting
and a desire to try
pride for a while.

Tears milked from gratitude
or the movement of song,
staying in one place
long enough to see
the right in wrong.

You have met your demons and
padded the sterile promentary.
Now is the time to join hands
with brave loved ones
around the simple table.
Call in your angels, and
summon momentum.

A scribbling in the dark.
A night time divination,
close to the source,
beyond all confusion.

Freedom and Forgiveness
(for B.R.)

Freedom and forgiveness
permission to promise.
Both granted now,
both needed too
for what you are
about to do.

Imagination will accompany
though no longer leads your
desire, for free and forgiven
you set out on the foothills,
your fiery headstrong stride
meeting the climb, its curve
lifting you.
Eyes fixed
breathing heavy rhythm,
reluctance relinquished.

You are powerful as the ocean.
Forgiven and free.

Chinook Sanctuary

Having descended into silence,
I face a wooden structure.
The Sanctuary breathes before me,
so I enter with rain on my skin.

Completely empty
it welcomes the emptiness
in me, called to prayer
the easy prayer of
simple breathing.

This is how a church should be,
the joining of warm wood together
making walls invisible, calling us
to join in, not leave behind
the life outside the door.

A church vulnerable
to fire and water,
a prayer vessel
floating in the forest.

Mesmerized by amber
tree lines ringing around me,
I knew courageous prayers
are said in places like this
with wood, not stone listening.

I knew utter joy sweeps
through places like these,
a shelter, not an escape.
Unfettered by damp rock and
twisted metal hidden behind
stained glass, lead lined
but a living, breathing
wild church, for
wild prayers.

And though the air is still,
a silent gale rows through
this singing space.
This silent cathedral
among the moss.
My skin thirsts again
for rain, my soul
a falling acorn, a
hazelnut floating.

Grant yourself refuge here,
grasp these sacred seconds,
and call your soul
your own.

The Mixed Blessing

It will be a long time
before you descend
to predictability. This
hall of mirrors becoming
the open plateau.

Things are beginning
to happen again.
Strange things,
solid synchronicities
which demand to be
thought of thrice.

The taste of metal
and rose petal aroma.

You thought you knew
what you wanted and
encouraged the best
in the folly.

Then that fell away,
leaving you standing,
knees shaking
close to buckling,
crying out before
the ends of sentences.

Your compass will still.
It is shuddering
to its pin point.

Over A Rainbow

Someday no matter
where you are,
a solitary song is
pure consolation.

Sing the hopeful anthem
under your breath to the
best of your ability, and
join this human chorale.
For you are not alone, but
one of many singing
this song, at this
very moment.

There could be one hundred,
there may be ten thousand
joining this private refrain.
A continuum that dares
to dream, we who have
committed this mantra
to memory wear this song
like a Garland.

Sharing our singing
space permits us
to hope against hope,
to wish upon wishes.

Stilling inner waters
to break our silence and
remind us, we will wake up
where blue sky seems to be
all God ever gave.

This promised land
we heard of once, is not
the stuff of lullabies
or happy little bluebirds,
for someone, somewhere
sings this song, and
someone, somewhere smiles
as they cease asking, 'why'?

Dark Sky

Stars are exquisite company,
making you a heavenly host.
The sky at night,
the dreamers' mirror,
making frail notions
of death seem juvenile,
and preposterous.

Stow away or
captain's mate, it
is too easy to deny
the soft buffetings
of life's bow, breaking
the waves of space
and time.

Do the stars tell us to
take our lives for granted?
Or are we aggrandized by
their scattered perfection?

Let us turn our lamps
down low, preserving
this divine horizon.
This place to celebrate
the glorious proof
our suspicions gift us.

The pure privilege
of not knowing,
the volatile wisdom
of letting.
The dark sky
is your life.

John's Poem

With my mother
in her home
by Chapel Lake.
You reading
her theology.

Or with Whyte
on Whidbey
by Puget sound.
You still wet
on his lips
and you dead
several years.

Or with my brother
on the M7, driving
through the Curragh.

I think of thee,
vast wisdom to pursue.
Permission can only be granted.
Our burden lain down at your feet
and imagine, just imagine.

The Virtuoso

I don't care if you're sorry,
nor do you even, anymore.
Why atone for your gifts?
Express remorse for
your ability, begging
pardon in public?

Be instead, the
unrepentant virtuoso!
For you choose to stand
showing us the spirit stir,
then fill and overflow
within you.

The spirit does not
ask forgiveness,
nor permission.
And upon your stage
you can do no wrong.

Get out of the way,
we love what you have
and need no reminder
of our sentence here
on earth, please,
just set us free.

LOVE

For My Father

The endless well
of celebration,
tectonic affection
and seismic loss
you are to me.

A different wing beat
now, a different wind.
Oh, why we die defines
how we must live
and love we did
and find, to stand
on holy ground we must
not talk too much, nor try
and know our own mind.

We were headed for the miracle,
but no matter now.
Time has made clear
what scans could not show.

'Allow space for celebration'
you are staring unblinking,
the healing icon,
my wandering eyes
on yours, our every tear
the same temperature,
come from the same place.

I always break you down
you say and I know
I hold the skeleton
key to your heart,
and now my own
heart too, I held it
all along, and finally
nowhere is out of reach
between us.

Of Love

Give in to it.
For when it's done
like this, hearts sing
and this couple hold us
in the hollow of their hands.

These beautiful two now
share the intimate
world to hide away
within each other.

A sacred space, a silence
in which they need,
not doubt.

They shall simply visit us
and wherever we are
we shall reflect
we realise they
are side by side.

But we can reach them now
no longer, for all is changed
and for the better.
Our treasured dearest one
is gone, the way it was
is gone and for the better,
for I was afraid of love
until I saw you
both together.

First White Hair

The thought of your eyes
heather brown,
make my pale blue
eyes glisten, and
I wonder how God
chose which strand
to grant your first
white hair.

You make an artform
of disappearance,
and teach me that life
is second nature.

I reach out at your request,
finding the strand between
my thumb and finger.
Stillness while you wait
for the pinch of the pluck.

Your eyes widen
as I rip the strand
from its root and realise
you are determined
to live, be free and
love what you love
unabashed, like a baby
in the shade,
gurgling.

Oh, most alive thing changing
before my eyes, let me change
with you, let your scalp be
the loom of my life, and
let your white hairs weave
a seam of double stitching
to bind us.

This silver strand
I hold is momentous,
for it is the last thread
I shall ever pluck
from your head.

And letting go of this white hair
in the warm and shining sun,
I watch it float upon the air
and turn with time,
and times begun.

She Sleeps So Deeply

She sleeps so deeply,
immediately and on demand,
can laugh hysterically
then announce
sleep's slow arrival.

Loving the slipping under
the glorious anesthesia,
suddenly she is surely gone.
Serene. Covered above
the shoulder, below the neck.

Though she still moves when
I move, as if to stay companion
to my wide eyed, nocturnally
turbulent sensibility.

So, I watch her doze
with a privileged air.
Wondering where my love
has gone, yet loving
this part of her life.
This heavy sedative
she so freely administers.

And when she wakes,
as she comes to, she speaks
from her place of dreamtime,
and with silly questions

or emphatic agreement,
can engage in conversation
or matter of fact description as if
it is I who has entered her world,
rather than me coaxing her
back to mine.

Tears in the Lane

Are you who I have waited for?
As you bring me to tears
in the lane among friends
and friendly clutter,
tears surprise my
eyes on contact.
I will fall deeper.

Tickled and treasured,
such hopeful devotion.
Elephantine loyalty,
I bow to your bow.
Tusk touching ground,
trunks entwined.

All awkward and sweet,
and stupid and beautiful.
I grieve my old life and
wonder what ancestors
make of our true love.

My future in your face,
your future in my eyes.
Our eyes welling up
ready for more,
tears in the lane.

Love Catches Up

Love catches up,
thanks be to God!
But weren't we marvelous
how we took our time to
not just let waters settle,
but let them fully still.

We read and breathed it
all together, blending family
like alchemists alloying
base metals into gold.
Willing the waters'
current return.

This day is a wisp
across the surface,
the depth of our
satisfaction is elemental,
tidal, our faces unable to
show our knowing glow.

So, a ritual was scheduled
and all came from several
parishes around to the old
ruined monastery, still
even more beautiful now
they ordain each other,
and you too!

Still water now no longer.
Still water now no longer carried.
New current returned and now
we're floating, carried along
to a meeting with yourself,
stepping out
onto Clonmacnoise.

Home of the Carers
(for Milford Hospice)

This is a home of carers
and care takes many forms.
This is a home of suffering
and suffering takes time,
and does its worst
while we wait
on both sides.

In this home we preen and preen
until strong feathers break
through air soft down, and
those ready fly away
as they may, any
moment now.

People die here, and
we die here with them.
The pain that lives
here is medicine
for the pluming,
a healing thing.

Day by day, we pass away
and nights are full
of letting go and
holding on, and
mornings do not break.
Here, they shatter into light.

Go Lassie, Go

If your true love should die,
would you surely find another?
You chose a body to love you,
astonished yourself by lust for flesh.
Fell in love with the mind within
and clung to them so tightly
to capture, and redeem
your own skin.

Your chosen mind,
this chosen flesh
now no longer here.
Dead to this world,
yet you and they
are still wedded.
Enslaved by their absence
humbled by love.

And we'll all go together
clutching flowers
of the mountain, for
within love's last rites
are powers to baptize
and love to be
born again.

BELIEF

This Is My Prayer Room
(for Maya)

This is my prayer room,
no one comes in.
I anoint icons here
with sandalwood and
pour milk over deities,
chanting a throaty mantra.

I sat cross legged
till I could no more
but don't worry,
my god already knows
my aches and pains.

This altar holds my trinkets
of faith, the tools of prayer,
instruments of hope
and rag offerings
to my elephant god.

If you wish to pray I'll let you,
turning halfway through
my rosary making sure
you are comfortable.
Tuesday's prayers are slightly longer,
you see.

The incense will rise for you and I,
for there is peace in worship

at the foot of a virgin mother
and a blue skinned baby.
The gurus and martyrs,
the saints and angels.

And when I hand you
the bell, ring it.
Not once, but
keep ringing till I tell you.

Pray with me, say the words,
ring the bell, we're almost there.
This part is my favourite,
it's where god feels the closest.
So ask for mercy, or for help,
or forgiveness, no need to tell.

For my story is your story,
is every body's story.

Let the bell stop ringing now.
We've prayed well today,
thank you for your silence.
I know my god is pleased
to meet you, sees your sad
eyes and sweet spirit
and knows you
have much more
to do.

Interfaith

Divinising
the space amid faith.
Ordinands with tears
and lips quivering.
That the minister
is in each one of us,
was unknown to me.

Ritual space,
where time slows
to an ecstatic drip,
and the breath of God
is as close as the slumbering
lover you love to listen to.

Now is the time
where we are stepping out
to grasp our rite to pass
the spirit blessing.

But, who is braver?
This new minister
or we, who dare to seek
their original blessing?

And to think
they do this for love.
For love, and love's time
has come.

Monk
(for M.P.H)

Miracles happen
Ausculta,
Rye smiling monk,
Kissing the darkness.

Prayer at dusk to a healing icon,
After vespers retreats,
Til night office, he
Revives his drooping spirit
Intoning Sanctus,
Carrying the line before him,
Knowing this part of eternity.

Hell hath no dominion,
Each soul selects her own society,
Dare not be caught in dormition, for
Eating the holy host,
Requires a fortitude of honesty,
Man taste God,
Absolute even when blinded,
Naturally, the monk has doubts.

Vespers with My Mother

Front row empty church
I tower over my mother.
She to my right,
I, on the aisle.

Forty monks onstage for Vespers.
My home and alma mater,
where we sing together.

When I was young, I never thought
we'd read the neumes in unison.
Her sotto voce just loud enough
to climb fives steps to the altar
and mix with the brethren.
Her sad solo line forever there
though barely invited.

Miracle Baby

I am the miracle baby,
ripe for your love,
timing my appearance
to my perfection.
Dote on me,
hold my foot and hand.
The universe pouring
into you.

I did not die or forfeit earth,
to grant you this chance
to raise and see me
live a life.

I had the chance to stay
with the ones you knew,
who have passed and
the bright ones I know,
who will follow
my surprise arrival.

Take me to your miracle
house, wipe miracle tears
from my miracle face.
I chose your plea
from the multitude,
for I find your heart
to be true, and your

family able for this
phenomenal child.

Take me with you now.
Don't leave me behind or
whisper near me to
shelter me from grief,
for I am the old soul
they speak of.

Often mistaken,
clueless and furious.
I will kindle the same in you.

Then, we shall reflect upon
the miracle day I found you.
This human child with you,
hand in hand.

Peak Fall

Where I come from
leaves fall from trees,
but here they linger and
speak before they die.

And it is rightly fêted
by all who wait
in trepidation,
for peak fall.

Peak fall
has a feeling
of shriving, and our
reluctance to enter
winter is summoned.

Vikings Sail Overhead

To get to Shannon airport,
take the tolled tunnel
under the Shannon river
as Vikings sail overhead.
They entered Éire on longship
through this proud estuary.

Shannon airport,
anathema to neutrality
still harbours longships,
near crewless vessels
en route to sail deserts
of the east, to loot
their monasteries.

Some longships carry Vikings home,
I've glimpsed their silent layovers.

This morning I set sail
from Shannon aiport, where
Vikings still sail through.
The curse of the gateway maybe, or
the curse of a nation so ancient
it fears of being forgotten.

Our place in Valhalla
is sure, to be sure.

Shame lies in that tolled tunnel
beneath the Shannon river,
where Vikings sail overhead.

Early Music

I learned to make music when I was alone,
revering the moment before I began
to sing, then break the solitary silence.

I learned to love my own voice,
making a friend of it, fashioning
a fountain pen to master
the phantom language,
each Brandenburg concerto
furrowing ground, turned up
loud, while my father drilled
his impossibly strong fingers
on the steering wheel,
careening the back roads
of Birdhill.

My mother would sing alone for hours,
Hildegard and sean nós, seamlessly sung.
Light would stream in the sash window
while she scribbled illegibly,
preparing for a performance.

I would drum my hands on my thighs
till they were hot and red, repeating
the same beat thousands of times,
honing the same phrase.

And in the evening we would gather
around two candles and

Early Music on cassette.
Before the dissonance and serialism,
an early music to keep us company.

An instrumental combination
to unlock conversation and
make the silences dance
like shadows in candlelight.

No vocal music to deflect and distract
from a small family huddled
around only food and flame,
and the warm faint sound
of wood and gut string.
Deepening every narrative,
sharing harmony and conversation.

A family that feels safe is sacred.
Embryonic echo soundings
still bounce back,
reflected in the sound
of Early Music.

The Bottom Line

Why do some believe
in themselves, above others?
And must the most careless
seem so blessed?
The most frugal, the least solvent,
the most visible, the least confessed!

You did not make this luck yourself,
your valued values parasitic infest,
those who have abundance gifted,
ye who feel abundance, blessed.

None among us are immune, for
a childish tyrant haunts our soul.
Though angels too our hearts control, and
the common promise of selfish things,
with our sacred interest brings us
one step closer to beggars, or kings.

Sometimes we must dance for rain
not plumb a well, but dance
for sun as well, for life
is not a march, but a
tidal, seasoned swell

What is in store whether rich or poor,
one reaching, weak, and final breath.
The bottom line won't give us more
for the bottom line in life,
is death.

WATER

Ballinahinch

Ballinahinch,
where the lurch of the water
caught me, then released me.
Hearing the silver trout jump
plump above the drizzle
at the bend of the river,
the castle on its bank.

Gráinne Mhaol left here
to become a pirate.
You leave here
to become a poet,
with blashts and
lightning raids
on meaning.

But what else will
this poor boy encounter?
How will he know
when this bend calls again?
And what if his mind is
numbed by drifting silt?
Will this unfolding river then
not inspire surprise?

I shall return to the river bend,
with the words that surfaced.

Catch and release that fish
I heard from that dark pool,
     deep and moving fast.

Swollen River

The quiet minute,
when sun goes low
after heat of day,
we searchers strike
out on the banks to
tickle, tease and lure
streamline spirits,
who grace the river beds.

Our quest endeavours
to come eye to eye
with the gasping animal,
Sunset still glowing on
its skin, then release it
to murky flooded waters
again, and again.

I know a man
who sits by rivers,
waiting for the plash
and telltale ripples.
Who gazes upon himself
with such patience, that
he does not need to tie
a single knot or disturb
the water's surface, for
he is forever fishing.

As his eye drifts the current,
the salmon summoned rises.
Taking, loud and strong his
finely feathered intention.

And as the heavy fish
wiggles down to stillness,
nosing the oncoming murk,
a fiery auburn spot appears
like a solar flare erupting,
from the silver of its belly.

Rain Poem

Soft rain,
wet rain,
sideways rain,
warm rain.

The taste of it dripping,
the privilege of standing in it,
not giving a damn.
Walking out under it,
underdressed and understanding
cloth is not the medium
conducive to conversation
with this most alive element.

Rain would run
off the skin if
it were let, and
skin rejoices when
padded by droplets.
Drinking the mist
like heather
sweetly blooming.

Let us give the knowing look,
hunch our shoulders
and scurry in the drizzle.
Lope through the torrent,
let harmless weather blow.

Leaving you damp and happier.
Readier for processed air, and
sealed tinted windows
of whatever institution
you thank deaf heaven
for having you…

Where you will yearn for rain,
and the smell of dirt,
wet rock, and a droplet
running down your back.

The Skylark
(for Patrick McCormack)

The skylarks beat their wings
over seven streams as
Sliabh na Glasha's panorama
is filling every vessel.

A farmer roars welcome
over his pride and joy,
'Do not underestimate the circumstances
that brought you here'.
To this clear source
above Glenquin.

Here, he brings
friends of friends who
seek the font of life.
Here, you are invited
to sign your name
in the sky above
Mulach Mór and leave
names of the dead
to swoop, and scream.

So that the steep descent
through hazelwood
to gingham laid lives seems
dangerously essential.

Frightened and girdered.
Happy and heartbroken.

A man named James
once watched me sing
while bright orbs
of blue and white rose
from that true source
of seven streams.

He whispered that to me.
I'm proud that I believe him.

Searching the glare for the skylark,
you find her call is ample, and
spying this animal in the sky
only amplifies the voice
you came here to silence.

Lower your eyes
from heaven to your horizon,
to the rocks you pad upon.
Listen to the hovering bird,
the skylark in the clear air.

Walk beneath it,
let this birdsong be
the twittering canopy,
a fluttering incantation

that calls forth the orbs
of blue and white to rise
up, out of water flowing
just beneath your feet.

Inis Cealtra / Holy Island

Standing on the shore,
Lough Derg is a glimmering danger.

Stepping into the fishing boat clumsily,
you are the monk ferried home.
Your habit's hem wet and heavy,
to the bright torch light
of Inis Cealtra.

Bittersweet is the return to exile.
To leave behind is to be taken in,
and you are part of this island
before ever setting foot
upon it again.

Your right hand trails
the water's warm surface.
Hungry for change, your praying
lately has only enflamed
old ways in you that lurk
like pike that swim
beneath you now
as you cross.

Retreat to your holy island,
where you begin again.
Returning lighter,
your habit's hem
pressed and flowing.

Step out from the fishing boat gracefully,
the round tower at your back.
Strike out carrying the lightest burden,
transformed from deep inside
and ready for the relief
of love.

MYTH

Lough Gur / Plunged Through

Two lads cutting rushes
plunged their sickle through it.
The hollow thud of bronze
unearthed ceremonial shield
and sun sign, offering
to the Goddess Áine,
who lives beneath Lough Gur,
watching the surface.

My grandmother conceived by this shore
and my mother was born.
But before that, Paddy and Nora
skated on the frozen lough
only for Nora to plunge through,
pulled up by the hair by
my grandfather after she
had already given up.

Nora maintained she felt
the Goddess Áine,
dragging her down
to her depths.
An enticing urge.

I can feel my grandmother
sinking in this lake,
letting go of her young love
and her future family, and
feeling that it could be

good to leave this world.
Confident in her savedness.

This prehistoric space, where
each undulation is a hoard, and
treasure lies among the rushes
once a holy offering.

Lough Gur beneath Knockaney,
Lough Gur beneath Knockadoon
that birthed my mother,
and spared hers.

Tuatha Dé Dannann

Spiritually inclined, we
were never to entertain
the bloody battle.
Our hearts quickened as
each shroud was broken
by serpentine bows.
Hollow hills beckon now,
they echo the slap of
Amergin's warship
on wave.

We are the dream of Éibhle.
We are the lick of the stream
trickling, the reason your
senses heightened.
We keep you safe,
standing out among
the peoples.

We are the ones
who stood the stones
that stand still.
We watch the bloody battles
and pray for peace.

Our ancient inclination
descending through
a spiritual strain.

Cuchulainn's Battle Fury
(From The Táin)

The Eldership were desperate and silent.
Upon his return he was dipped in barrels
but to no avail, his riastrach frightening
his joints, twisted and gnarled in agony.

Now his mind is gone, and we
must touch the arrow point
of his weapon to pacify
this warrior, for we need
this mighty man.

So Cúchulainn was approached
by the women, breasts revealed.
Convincing the animal psyche
of its own birth and the love
now at the sea bed of his heart.
His genius clouded and sodden with
the blood of the northern queen
and all the souls in between.
He was calmed
by the final feminine gesture.

Famous for his battle fury,
valor and skill, and the way
he heals from deep gashes
so quickly, his battle fury
so strong only the womb
reminder made him

ours again.

The eldership still petrified
as the power of peace
bares its breast.

The Shoulders of Enbar
(for the mosaic in St. James' Hospital
by the artist Nicholas Kinney)

Life's piecing together.
Fragments furnaced,
coloured, blown, broken
and fastidiously glued.
Creates mosaic,
living's ancient artform.

Imagine the delight
when glass was tamed,
shaped, and dyed.
The alchemical shimmer
touching our eyes,
hungry for colour
and flowing movement.

Our fascinations frozen
as time slips away.
Glass, marble and gold leaf
side by side, above
and below one another.
An otherworldly invitation
to the still point.

The muses manifested at St. James'
are Oisín and Níamh.
A narration of young love
and life's shortness.

Lifted onto the strong
shoulders of Enbar,
they whisk away
to Tir na nÓg.

This artform keeps us young.
And for a time we dare
not look away.
But we too must pine
and retreat to home
in time, again on
Enbar's strong shoulders.

Breaking the eye's mosaic embrace,
we dismount the magic carrier.
Our feet again on Irish soil,
thanking God three hundred
years have not passed since
our unblinking passage.

For no land beyond
time stops the longing
for the fellowship of ageing,
and each time we return
from Tir na nÓg, we sense
we've been away
too long.

Ferdia and the Gáe Bolg

Foster brothers,
they sent healing
herbs across the ford
during the darkness.

On the fourth morning
Cúchulainn prepared
his secret spear.
Renowned weapon,
Gáe bolg.
Which, once it enters
must be cut out, quickly
filling the bloodstream
with its barbs, the spear
made from the bone
of a sea monster.

Hurled over water
from the fork of the foot
of Cúchulainn, only
then would its ritual
power be divined.

Scáthach's spear
was launched and
met its mark, Ferdia
dies severely.

Hero or coward be,
our fiercest weapon
we keep for our kin.

My Father Plays

Awaken and listen
my father plays,
harp music
on pianoforte.

Waking up to proud
struts instilled in
the courtly tunes of
Bonaparte's crossing
and farewell to music,
are right hand ornaments
and left hand figured bass.

Truly, it is the hero's music
of what happens, worthy
of Ború's court, or
Fianna's fireside.
My father plays still,
swimming in tradition.
The Gaels can hear it,
demand it, still justly bitter
but wistful now once more.

For music brings the dead
back to this island.
We entered into contract,
habitation at a price.
Paid, gladly.